# ELI
## Goes to
# Church

ISBN 978-1-68570-312-7 (paperback)
ISBN 978-1-68570-313-4 (digital)

Copyright © 2022 by Josh Knipple

All rights reserved. No part of this publication may be reproduced, distributed, or transmitted in any form or by any means, including photocopying, recording, or other electronic or mechanical methods without the prior written permission of the publisher. For permission requests, solicit the publisher via the address below.

Christian Faith Publishing
832 Park Avenue
Meadville, PA 16335
www.christianfaithpublishing.com

Illustrated by: Thyra Jacobs

Printed in the United States of America

# ELI
## Goes to
# Church

JOSH KNIPPLE

ILLUSTRATED BY THYRA JACOBS

It's Sunday morning.

"Time to wake up, buddy."

"Why, Daddy?" Eli whines.

"It's time for church, bud," Daddy replies.

"Oh yeah, that's right," says Eli with a sigh.

(*Eli gets ready and asks.*)
"Daddy, why do we go to church?"

"To learn all about God!" Daddy exclaims.

"That's right, Daddy! Now I remember," Eli says.

(*At church, as Eli and his family walk in, the greeters shake their hands, saying,*) "Goooood morning, Eli!"

"Mommy, who are those people?" Eli asks, confused.

Mommy replies, "Those are the greeters—to make you feel welcome."

"Like family?"

"Exactly!" Mommy responds.

"I like the greeters! They do a good job!" Eli declares loudly.

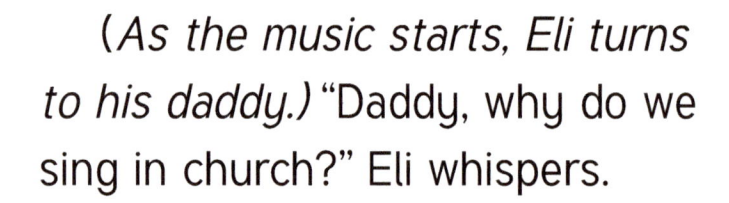

(*As the music starts, Eli turns to his daddy.*) "Daddy, why do we sing in church?" Eli whispers.

Daddy whispers back, "It's our way to tell God we love Him."

"Like I tell you and Mommy I love you?" Eli asks.

"You got it, buddy."

"Okay, Daddy!" Eli says, as he starts to sing louder.

"Will you join me in prayer?" the pastor asks.

"What does it mean to pray, Mommy?" Eli asks, confused.

"Prayer is our way to talk to God."

"Just like I'd talk to you?" asks Eli.

"You got it, little man!" says Mommy.

"Mommy, now I get it!" Eli exclaims, as he smiles away.

(*After prayer, the pastor continues.*) "Please open your Bibles."

"Daddy, what's the Bible?" Eli asks, confused.

"It is God's Word for us," Daddy replies.

"God's Word?"

"Yep, God's story for you and me."

"Okay, Daddy," says Eli. "Now I get it."

"What are we doing now?" Eli asks.

"The pastor is going to teach us," says Mommy.

"Like my teacher in school?"

"Yep, that's right."

"Sounds good! I love to learn!" Eli says, smiling again.

"Now go be the light!" the pastor shouts.

"What does be the light mean, Daddy?" Eli asks on the way home.

"It means to live out what you learned, to be like Jesus, and to do the things that He would do," Daddy explains.

"So I should try to be like Jesus and do what the Bible says in my life?" Eli asks.

"Exactly!" Daddy replies, smiling.

"Good idea, Daddy, I like that!" Eli exclaims.

"Daddy, I've been thinking," Eli states, excited.

"What's on your mind, li'l man?"

"I want to try to be the light."

"Yeah? That's a big challenge," Daddy explains. "Are you up for it?"

"I know I am. Just like my night-light shines in my room, I want to shine!" Eli says even more loudly.

"I love you, buddy. Now get some rest."

"I love you too, Dad," Eli says while shutting his eyes.

"You have a big day tomorrow living like Jesus," Daddy whispers, as he shuts the door.

(*Next day on the bus to school*) "Can I sit with you?" Eli asks the kid sitting all alone.

"Who, me?" the little girl asks, surprised.

"Yep!" Eli proclaims.

"Okay," the kid replied, smiling. "But why?"

"Because Jesus told me I'm to treat others how I want to be treated."

(*Eli gets knocked over on the playground.*) "Hey, that's mine!" Eli yells, as his ball goes flying.

The kid then laughs and pushes Eli over.

Eli sits a moment, then says surprisingly, "I forgive you."

Surprised, the bully asks, "Why? I popped your ball."

"Jesus told me to forgive like He forgave me," Eli says, happy as he can be.

(*Eli shares his lunch.*) "You can have some of mine," Eli proclaims.

"Are you sure? Aren't you hungry?" the kid questions.

"Yes, but so are you."

"Why are you so nice to me?"

"Jesus says to give to those in need," Eli states, knowing he had just made a friend.

(*Back home*) "How was your day, buddy?" Daddy asks, as Eli gets home.

"Awesome, Daddy! I got to be like Jesus!" Eli shares, excited.

"Oh, yeah?" Mommy asks.

"Yep," said Eli. "I sat with a kid all by herself, I shared my lunch, and I even forgave a kid for knocking me over."

"Now aren't you just a funny kid." Daddy laughs.

"Faith like a child!" Mommy shouts.

"I think we should celebrate." Daddy smiles.

(*The following Sunday*) "You know what, Daddy?"

"What's that, Eli?" Daddy asks.

"I love Sundays! I think it's my favorite day of the week," Eli answers.

They both smile and start laughing.

Eli goes to church!

**The End**

# About the Author

Josh is a full-time missionary for Crucified Ministries and Snowboarders and Skiers for Christ (SFC). He is married to the love of his life, Lindsey, and together they have four children: Eli, Silas, Elliston, and Evans. Having kids truly gave them a new perspective on God's love and grace.

Josh and his family live in Western Pennsylvania and have a heart for the outdoors and a passion for seeing others come to faith in Christ.

CPSIA information can be obtained
at www.ICGtesting.com
Printed in the USA
BVHW060405241022
649930BV00001B/1